Lost in Burma

Lost in Burma

"Queenie"
and 50 other war poems

R.E. Maloney

SPIDER BOOKS
PUBLISHING

This book may be ordered through booksellers or by contacting:

Spider Books Publishing, LLC
PO Box 51911
Fort Myers, FL 33994
www.SpiderBooksPublishing.com
(239) 693-DRAW (3729)

ISBN: 978-1-942728-11-5 (Print)
ISBN: 978-1-942728-12-2 (Digital)

Printed in the United States of America

Editing: Robert Maloney
Cover design: Rachel Olson
Book design: Jennifer FitzGerald - www.MotherSpider.com
Cover image copyrights at DepositPhoto.com and 123rf.com

The Author and Whitey.

We later called it the 'Ten Years After Photo'. It was taken 10 years after Shanghai, in the summer of 1955.

We met in Kunming, China, in March, 1945, re-enlisted in the U.S. Army in Shanghai in November. For most of our 3-year enlistment period, we were together in several German postings, including Erlangen, Bad Nauheim, Kassel, and Wetzlar.

This book of poems is dedicated to Whitey, who passed away 10 years after this picture was taken. No better friend has any man ever had.

PREFACE

I will probably have reached, and passed, my ninety-first birthday by the time you read through these poems. I can almost guarantee you will:

      1) like a good many of them,
      2) cry a couple of times and,
      3) laugh at least now and then.

Many, probably fifteen or more, stem from my experiences while serving with the US Army in the China-Burma-India Theatre of War between November of 1944 and December of 1945.

Some others come from my experiences at, and about, a wonderful Nursing Home in Ft. Myers, Florida. This during a 10+ year period while my wife was a dementia-stricken resident. She passed away in August 2014, and I now spend my time writing.

Again, I hope you enjoy each and every poem as much as I enjoyed writing them.

- Bob Maloney

Note: Of this group of poems, only Cadillac Kate and The Five and Dime have been previously published.

Contents

Lost in Burma

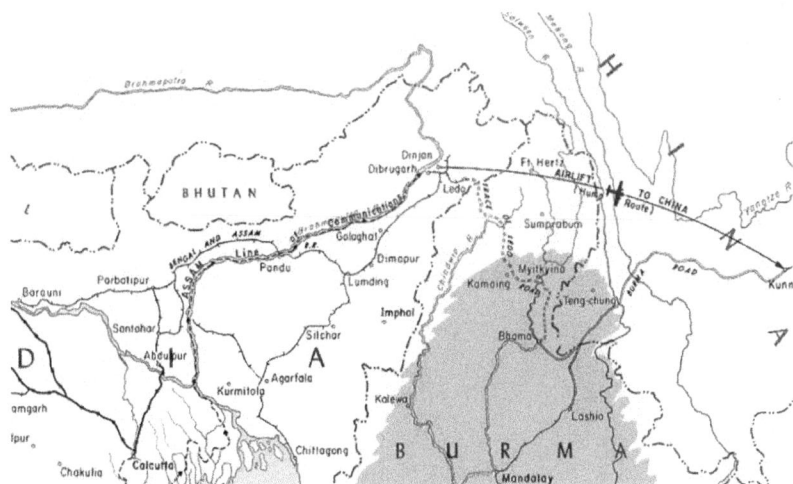

The Burma Road

Cadillac Kate

From behind the bed/chair, I could see the red hair
And she didn't really look that great.
Then she opened her eyes, and to my surprise,
I was looking at Cadillac Kate!

It was back in eighty-two that Katie joined the crew
At the regular Friday Night Meeting.
I recall her sailing in, wearing a sly grin,
And then kissing us all in her greeting.

She said, "I just got here, 'tho my car threw a gear
And is back in a Georgia shop."
We were all enthralled, and as I recall,
She'd left it with a Valdosta cop.

Well, she flew to Valdosta (God knows what it cost her)
And picked up her car, and her cop.
So that's how Kate got her new name and buddy;
But, now it was about her last stop.

As I reminisced, she asked to be kissed,
So I came close to her cheek, and said, "Kate."
I touched her bare shoulder, felt it get colder,
But my kiss, alas, was too late.

At which point I looked up, and there holding a cup
Of what looked like a warm cup of tea,
A nurse shedding a tear, saying, "Excuse me dear,
But that lady was named Anna Lee."

The Corner of
Medford and Sycamore

One corner of Medford and Sycamore
Had a broken down shack of a variety store.
Luckies were two for a penny then;
Thank God, I couldn't buy many then.
I'm almost glad I was poor!

But, Somerville, Mass. was really a gas
Before Hitler and Tojo showed up,
Corners at twilight, bread was a nickel
But the world was about to erupt.

Across the street was the corner of choice,
Where the nightly editions lay,
THUD, off the back of a newspaper truck
Quick! How'd the Sox due today?

The cop on the corner of Medford and Sycamore
Was a guy I remember so well,
We called him Officer Powell
And he loved us kids, you could tell.

The corner was always crowded
At eight, and again at three,
That's when kids were coming and going
To the Foster School, you see.

Sometimes our policeman would put up his hand
And four cars would squeal to a stop,
While Officer Powers put some kid on his shoulder
And crossed the street hippity-hop.

About five, or six, as evenings got on
It was the teens and guys time to boast,
Sharing their day, talking about Foxx
And this Williams kid, up from the coast.

What might Louis do to Schmeling?
The next time these fighters met,
Could Cronin turn the Sox around?
The older guys said, "You bet!"

Did you see who took the sixth today?
Some nag from upstate New York,
Now, if the fix wasn't in on that one,
I'll swim back to County Cork.

Then one morning everything halted,
It was Monday, in a cold December,
Pearl Harbor had been bombed, the navy sunk,
And every kid there would remember.

Steve

There he sat, unable to drive,
Sipping a beer and still alive.
His leg in a cast,
Pondering his past,
It was even money he'd not survive.

One thousand miles, he had come
"Finally made it; hi ya, Mom!
Got a ride right from Daytona.
Not much fun, bein' a loner,
Not much fun, bein' a bum."

The trucker who brought him,
A guy Steve called Slim,
Said, "I saw the two canes,
So I slid over two lanes;
I guess it was done on a whim!"

Well, Steve did stick around
But then finally headed west-ward bound,
Hobbling, but now with only one cane;
There he was, on the road again,
Headed for another, more lively, town.

Six months later, a ringing phone;
I thought it had another tone;
And it did, because, out of the blue
And somehow Evie had a clue;
Steve was saying, "I'm no longer alone."

He said her name was Diane,
And they were working on a plan;
To get clean and sober together;
They were surely birds of a feather.
Evie said, "And with God and AA, you can!"

Our CNAs

Wiggle, Wiggle down the hall,
How I love you, one and all.
Some are wide, some are tall,
Some like a fish-pole, some like a ball.
Hustling along, hair in a fall;
How I love you, one and all.
Some are steadies, some on call,
Some like music; (they all like the mall!).

These are my cuties
Always doing their duties,
And never pleading for praise;
These, my friends, are our CNAs.
Wiggle, wiggle down the hall
These girls who give me life;
For you see, they are a part of me.
They take care of my beautiful wife.

Our Nurses

Wan big tuffes' job,
In all 'dis crazee worl,
Whether you big Russian guy
Or wee little Irish gurl.
Is standin' on your feet all day
At a shaky nursing station
Pounden lil' pills to dust
An wachin' 30 pations.

All de while she got in mine
Another can soon be gawn,
An she'll be doin' paper work
And tryin' not to mawn.
She luv them all pretty much you see;
Dere's no time to relax
And she has no time to tink aboud
Wah dis Romney guy pays in tax.

Evie and the Dental Lady

A few short days past eighty-five,
And strange as it seems, I'm still alive
And you know why I think that's so funny?
'Cause nobody knows I'm outa money!

Every month, a laughing, tubby, lady
Leans over and kisses my cheek;
Then she says, "Evie, my sweetie,
Open up and we'll have a peek."

She brushes away, all huffy and puffy
(My God, this woman is big;)
But, gentle and chatty, maybe a mite catty;
(I wonder how she got this gig?)

The dental inspection now over, she says,
"Evelyn, everything's just duckie."
The lady then ties a plastic bag
To my wheelie and I really feel lucky.

Not that I've got a brand new toothbrush
(A bright red one), for the next thirty days.
But Chubby didn't even give me a bill;
Well, I guess My Bobbie pays.

Evie

You're starting to get some wrinkles, Hon,
Right here by your little chin;
Now I know there's only just a few,
But, you didn't have any
When you were eighty-two

Winter 1932

Chet and my brother
Were goofing around,
When Richard slipped
On the frozen ground.

When Richard got up
He was spilling blood;
To my little brain
It looked like a flood.

We all went inside,
To find some bandages,
And have dear old Mom
Assess the damages.

Mom poured clear stuff
Along Richard's arm;
I just knew how it stung,
But my brother stayed calm.

When the wound was clean
Mom kissed his tousled head;
Then the kid asked her quietly,
"Why is blood red?"

Isaac

De sky, she's grey like very old man,
Maybe real Isaac look dis way;
And de wind get blowin' and sticky
And de mailman don't come today.

Pretty soon I see a baseball hat;
He's bounce alon' de street;
Some old fart give chase de hat
Wid big slippers on his feet.

I yell, I tell him, go back home
De win' gonna' git real bad,
Dat when he hit de banana peel
And com down right on his had.

Now, some guys lose a rug or two
And cars don wanna start,
But how many loos a base ball hat,
Like dis crazy guy old fart?

The Future

I asked my kid, "Ever think in rhymes?"
He came back, "Well, I guess, sometimes."
"And do you ever write them down?"
He said, "What for?" with a little frown.

"So you won't forget them; maybe they're good;
You may have some talent; maybe you should,
How 'bout a sample; give it a try."
He said, "OK, here's one 'on the fly'."

*"I love senior math class
'Cause there's this babe with a great ass
Keeps looking in my direction
With what I hope is great affection"*

("Son, that's what I call class!")

Whitey

I was lying in bed in a Kunming tent
My nurse was a Burmese beauty;
She said , "You really velly sick."
I said, "And you are really some cutie!"

There's a guy in the next bed,
Says, "It's called lack-a-nookie."
The nurse giggled a bit, and then asked,
"Would you like some milk and maybe a cookie?"

"The doctor," she said, "he 'dink mararia.
I tell him, I don dink so;
I see whole bunch in India,
But here in China, I dink No."

Ten days later they let me out,
They never did make a diagnosis;
One said pneumonia, another malaria
Another made no prognosis.

Heading for the walled city,
I see this guy from the next bed
He asked, "Was she right?
I didn't catch what the new doctors said."

"Don't ever give blood," the Doc told me.
"But a pound of sulfur helped, I guess."
He asked if I could drink, yet,
I said, "Let's give it the ultimate test."

While drinking the night away,
As we cruised from joint to joint,
He told me about his outfit;
Then came straight to the point.

"You're going back to Ledo
What, to ride in another convoy?
Why not ask for a transfer
So my Captain can jump for joy!"

"We need a company clerk, Bob,
And you'd love it here in Kunming;
We've got a helluva mess hall,
And wait till you see the Cling Ting!"

Fort Myers International

The airport we use is pretty big;
Real International and such,
But, I heard the guys in security
Aren't always doing too much.

In fact, the paper says a bunch got fired,
(About 20 percent, it said)
That means a bunch of slots are open,
And they pay pretty good, it read.

Well, I took myself to the airport
Hoping I might get picked,
But I think I goofed with my question:
"Do the stewardesses get frisked?"

A Slow Boat to China

South of Hawaii, five thousand troops, and
Out there, somewhere, little island groups;
A lot of ocean is in between
Hiding killer subs, that can't be seen.

South of Perch; we made it this far,
Can we get a beer, maybe a cigar?
"Soldier Boy," the top kick said,
"We sit here long, and we'll all be dead."

South of Bombay, they tell us more;
In twenty-four hours we'll go ashore;
Thirty-one days, half of them on deck, and
Most of us have turned insomniac.

South of Ledo, and the Burma Road;
Eight days by train, plus a river boat.
We crossed the Ganges, boat after boat,
One kid asked, "You sure this will float?"

South of Kunming, (that's in China, you know)
Where the Flying Tigers, under Chennault
Were doing their thing to help;
And finally, our war was about to begin.

Errant Arrow

I think there's a Mall on West Street,
At least there was a few years ago;
(I'm talking about Keene, New Hampshire)
And folks there will probably know.

But no doubt there's only a few,
Who knew the place in nineteen thirty-one;
It was then a textile mill, you see,
(And unlike the mall, not a whole lot of fun.)

But right next door was a red brick house
Where lived Old Dick Keyes with his clan;
Grandpa Keyes was Mill Super, you see,
(Though I hardly remember the man.)

I do remember the house's back yard;
Right close by the railroad tracks;
We used to play there once in awhile
(Even took some hardball whacks!)

But, this day there were only three of us;
Me, my brother and Chet Whittle;
My brother and Chet were about 12,
But, I was still pretty little.

We each had a bow and arrow;
Home made, but that didn't matter,
The arrows could go quite a distance
(And made Gramp's dogs skittet-scatter).

Late afternoon, we're looking west,
Standing side-by-side;
I looked up to shoot my arrow,
Whap! I got one in the eye.

The Massachusetts Eye and Ear Infirmary
Is in Boston, about 70 miles away,
With Mom and Dad, I'm on a train;
(I guess the mood was pretty gray.)

The next day, after tests and other opinions,
They all agreed, nothing could be done;
In a year or two, that eye would go blind
And I'd have to get along with just one.

Fast forward to March, nineteen forty-three
The physical is over, what will they say?
Then one of the two Majors at the table says,
"Son, if you want in, you'll be sworn in today."

Old Toes

My gran-dotter say, how do you feel?
I say, "Pretty damn gud, was de deal?
She say you pushin' big nine-o
I say, hon, is not good time to go, so
Don't even tink about cook las' meal!
       And,
My VA quack sez my BP's high
Too much salt, he sez, tha's why
He say, any day I catch a stroke;
(And I don't tink this old fart joke)
I say, OK, I give a try.
        I hear,
War mart sell BP machine, OK?
I dink is fifty I have to pay
Get it home, looks easy to do
Holy scheissen, ---one eighty two!
And you dink *you* had a crappy day?
        So,
Da VA put me on a cell phone leesh
I gotta call and speak my piece;
"Did you take you meds today?"
Then, "Punch in one, or you can say,
Yes or no," (this way they teach)
       Lady say,
"Like 'tro your sal' shaker oud da trash"
I say to phone, "Go kiss my ass!"
Any way, I trow out de soups,
Dey in de lousy sodium groups,
She say, all good stuff, I gotta pass.

Take,
Gravy, ice cream; all gotta go,
And, no more salt, on de boil potato;
He say, "Eat oatmeal, every day."
I say, "You wanna live dis way?"
Say, "Is up to you." And I say, "Hell no"
But,
'Bout two AM, I come wide awake
Big toes stiff like garden rake
I get outta bed, but pain too much
Maybe call Corky; he ain't far.
Fall down de floor, try to touch
and
My toes; maybe give good shake
Finly gat up but not so far
Got to gat to de friggin' car;
Gat far as de sofa, better rest
Try to tink wha' might be best
maybe
Was last I think, before I doze,
That no good, 'cause I suppose,
It middle of nite, all guys asleep
So I pass out, wid out a peep
Not dinkin' about de big hot toes.
Now
Is sis oclock and de sun she shinin'
And wid it I'm see-in a silver linin';
My toes are all like dey was before
My old skinni ass hit de dam floor
So now, dear God, can I jus quit whinin?

The Troop Train

The train was freezing cold,
To say nothing about the troops!
We broke down somewhere near Denver
Now we're standing around in groups.

They said it might be an hour or two;
(That translated to four or five)
We're wondering how the General thought
We'd get to Utah alive.

We'd started from Abilene (Texas)
In the winter of '43, '44;
Headed, we knew not where,
Or what might be in store.

Then a brakeman told us 'Ogden'
That's where they would unload,
So A guy named Harry Huff said,
"Fuck it; let's hit the road."

Two days later we're in the bar
Of Ogden's Ben Lomond Hotel;
Huff had just decked some guy
And I caught him as he fell.

The scene was crazy, as 20 drunks
Were having one last drink;
We knew our days were numbered,
We'd soon be in the clink.

Well, the Lord looks after idiots
'Cause some guy with nothing to gain,
Said, "Look there by the station,
I think that's maybe your train!"

And, sure enough, there it was
And Huff said, "I see my car."
So off we went to see what's what
But we didn't get very far.

Comin' from what was our train
Was Swetka, looking mad as hell
He was our big first sergeant
(I wasn't feeling so well.)

"I don't want no excuses," he spat.
"Now, get back on the train;
Forget about any week-end pass
And don't pull that shit again!"

A Slow Truck to Kunming

We weren't looking for Lisu
Or Kachins or the Li.;
No, they found us Americans
When we stopped for a little spiked tea.

They came down from the mountains,
Maybe a hundred, maybe two;
To touch our trucks, and hands;
Speaking a language no one knew.

They wrote symbols, in the dirt,
Asking, "Who are you, why you here?"
All were small, many had goiters;
None showed an ounce of fear.

We couldn't stay long with our new friends;
(Who had never heard of the U.S. A)
None had ever seen a white man,
But they even asked us to stay.

But, with one hundred forty trucks,
And hundreds of miles yet to go,
(Plus a couple of ambulances)
We knew it would be really slow.

Hammocks, spread between trucks,
Had to do, for fourteen nights;
Two blankets under, four more over;
Incredibly, there were no fights!

The nights, at 12,000 feet, were freezing;
The days were sunny, almost hot;
We were the third convoy to make it
And no one even got shot!

Father Casey

Father Casey said, "I'm getting tired,"
Telling his dad his woes.
"My Bishop says I could get fired,
Even my mistress knows."

"Well, if it's only money, John,
I might have a good idea;
Might even get you promoted;
And get you out of here."

That Sunday morning after Mass,
Father Casey addressed his Clan:
All parishioners would get Last Rites
Early, on a monthly payment plan.

Not only that, he went on to say,
We can put a rider to the deal;
With a guaranteed, pre-paid, burial
In our own little lily field.

Well, the Bishop showed up
The following day
To send the good Father
On his merry way

No, not back to Boston
Or Tahiti or Haynes City;
Instead, Father Casey was now,
The new Walter Mitty

You see, when the final word
Was leaked from Rome,
We heard Father John O. Casey
Had found a new home

And where, you might ask
Did the Bishop dispatch
The good Father Casey
And what was the catch?

Why, to the Vatican, of course
To work for the Pope,
To become the new Treasurer,
And the new White Hope.

Joe

While taking a whiz, Joe got a call;
To meet his sweetie at the mall;
He had to hurry because it was late,
And he'd never anger his little mate;
But his day soon did a rotten cropper
When he dropped his Apple down the hopper.

The Sword

When you're a couple years short of ninety,
And you still get chills from a slinky nightie,
Then it's time to stand up and say:
Honey, it's been a great day.
Now, let's see if the sword is still mighty!

A Loan

"Psst, got a ten I can borrow?
I'll have it back by tomorrow."
I slipped him the bill under the table
When it's your kid, can you not enable;
Even when it leads to more sorrow?

Medicare

You can take my old rocking chair;
Raise my rent; what do I care?
You're right, 'not much'
Unless you touch,
One silver hair of my Medicare

Getting Better

Like the newest of babes, she lay there asleep
Tremors now gone, my feelings run deep.
Suddenly her eyes are glued to mine,
A tiny smile confirms her thought;
No, she cannot speak it, but I can feel it,
Another moment that could never be bought.

Thal's Place

Even if you lived in Shanghai,
In October of forty-five,
You'd probably never heard of Thal's Place,
Now let me tell you why.

Thal's was like no other joint
(Don't talk to me of 'Rick's')
Sure, there were a few cute ladies,
Ready to turn some tricks.

But you mainly met survivors
Russian, Jews, some Sikhs;
Other Asians, here and there;
Maybe an Aussie, or couple of Greeks.

The place was down an alley
Off a one way street;
One used only by rickshaws
And unknown to American MPs.

You had to climb a flight of stairs,
And then a shorter set,
That opened on a very odd scene
As weird as it could get.

Music came from a radio;
Wagner and Mozart, I think;
Suddenly, a glitter-gowned lady appears;
"Would you guys like a drink?"

The bar was a kitchen table,
In fact there were five or six;
"Help yourself," she offered;
There's gin and beer and mix.

Most of the people, 30 or so,
Were dressed as you would expect;
Including the Colonels and Majors
Most you would easily forget.

A donation punch bowl was sitting there,
One that was surely the real thing,
I was even tempted to flip my finger,
And give it the testing 'ping'.

The bowl was full of money;
Rupees, rubles, marks and yen,
Bills from all around the world;
All places I'd never been.

The Glitter Lady made use of the roof
To entertain the chosen.
They said she did it standing up;
And stiff, like someone half frozen.

My friend, Whitey was most curious,
But I said, "I think I'll pass."
Then Whitey said, what's that smell, Bob?
Almost like Kunming; it sure ain't regular grass."

No, this was opium and very close;
Some guy said it was three doors down;
Third bedroom on the left, he said.
Thal's had the best in town.

By late October the place was closed;
A Navy Lieutenant was found dead;
Stuffed down the building's chimney
"Got rough with Glitter," they said.

In some ways, Thal's was just a snapshot
Of a metropolis right after the war;
But make that metropolis Shanghai,
And think of the Dragon's Claw!

Hongkew

It was called the Hongkew District
A place to dine, drink and get high
On the river that led to the Pacific
In the choas we called Shanghai.

We'd dropped the bomb, and now,
All knew they'd be no invasion;
What followed the Nippon surrender
Was an All-World celebration.

It was October, nineteen forty and five
Some Japanese soldiers walking around
Guns slung with their knapsacks,
Asking, "Where do we to go aground?"

In the midst of all this commotion,
Two refugees named Angus and Small
Made more noise with dueling banjos
Than a Birmingham Gospel hall.

Angus played strictly by memory
He picked up his songs in a flash,
And played Old country ditties,
And dragged in the motley cash.

Smalley would switch to his drums
He was from being a Pro
So pick away, bang away anyway
Let's just get on with the show.

The girls sat around on bar stools,
Inviting us to buy the champagne;
Bottles that had Russian labels,
And tasted like sugar cane.

The girls, of course, would come and go
While Angus and Smalley played on,
Ochichornia requested, over and over;
Then, one day, they all were gone.

We found the place all boarded up
And not a soul in sight;
A couple of minutes later,
An MP came into sight.

He told us the place had been a plant
That Angus and Small were spies, or such;
That our OSS was also involved,
And they'd worked, he thought, for the Dutch.

Do you think that came as a big surprise?
Well, not in Shanghai in late '45
Where you guarded your Army meal card,
And watched your ass after five!

The Cling Ting Café

My new friend, Whitey, led me astray!
He dragged my ass to the Cling Ting Café;
We'd met in a proper Kunming bar,
Drinking spiked tea from a samovar.
It didn't take long 'till we headed out
To some special place he'd heard about;
It was in the Walled City, about a mile away
Patrolled by MPs, both night and day.

But this was neither, being half past five;
Sun still up, joints closed, not yet alive;
Finally got pointed in the right direction
By a young MP who knew this section.
"The Cling Ting? Not open yet," he said.
"But go around the back by the wooden shed;
A cutie named Queenie will let you in.
A pack of ciggies gets you rice wine or gin."

The place had a bar along one wall
Tables with phones, you wanna make a call
To one of the ladies you like as a mate;
If that was Queenie, you'd have to wait.
But, when Whitey asked, she came right over
And Whitey felt he'd soon be in clover.
But Queenie said, while sitting on his lap
"I solly soljer, I tink I got some clap."

I figured Whitey would send her away;
Go somewhere else, or another day;
But Whitey put out his arms as if to engulf her
And said, "Don't worry kid, I'll get you some sulfur!"
This was June, nineteen forty-five
I doubt if the Cling is around anymore
Nor is my best friend still alive;
A bad ticker killed Whitey in '65.

Queenie

Whitey saw the girl in a bamboo cage,
Her chin at rest on her knee;
He thought she looked familiar
And said, "I guess I'd better go see."

Sure enough, that was Queenie, all right,
His 'friend' from the Cling Ting Café
The one who stood about 4 foot ten;
(Whitey was six foot three)

Well, Queenie spoke a little English,
But, to Whitey, she acted dumb,
And like she didn't know him;
She was quiet, still; almost numb.

Then a Chinese guard with a pole came along,
Which he pushed into the cage
And he growled as he started poking
Which sent Whitey into a blinding rage.

The Chinese guy was Queenie's size
Maybe five feet one, no more;
And Whitey hit the guy so hard
It broke the little cage door.

Queenie came out like a shotgun blast
With nary a 'thank you please',
And while I was watching her disappear,
Here come the fuckin' MPs

So, while they were cuffing Whitey
And getting names and such,
Whitey said, "Maybe you can find her, Bob;
Tell her I'll be in touch."

Two nights later at the Cling Ting Café
I spotted her through the haze;
I sidled up close, and said, "Queenie, Hon,
Poor Whitey got fifteen days."

Bronski

It was clear as a bell at Kunming Field;
Just about three miles away;
And buzzing the field like hornets;
Some Japs were busy at play.

Their wings had big red circles
Just so we would all know;
They were there to raise some holy hell,
While they zipped around to and fro.

All this time our sirens scream;
"Get yourselves to the fields!"
(Where just last week we'd got ready
For one of these sneaky deals.)

So Bronski spilled his cup of gin
Then grabbed at a pile of clothes
And we all weren't a long way back
Except Whitey who was 'indisposed.'

We hit the trenches like drunken cats
Falling from a cypress tree;
All except Bronski who said,
"I gotta go back, I can't see."

Well, you shoulda seen the two of 'em;
Whitey looking scared and coming fast;
Bronk heading the other way,
Shouting at Whitey, as he went past.

Whitey came in like he was stealing second,
And yelling stuff I cannot mention;
Then just as Whitey got himself zipped,
A big loud boom really got our attention

We all thought Bronk forgot his glasses;
But those we would later find;
No, it was something much more important:
It was his Camels, he'd left behind.

The Robber

Dis guy cum in my ole book store
Big pockets in his coat,
An' one side hang like down a foot;
My brain, she make a note.

I don' tink dis guy gut his lunch
Or, bottle of booze, maybe gin;
Hiding in de black raincoat,
And he's got dis big dark grin.

I say good day, how do you do,
He say he jus' wanna chat;
That when I point to door; he bit,
And I swing my baseball bat.

I catch de basta side de had,
He go down like some big stone;
I bend over dis crazy bum,
I don' hear any some groan.

So I gat my phone, call nine one one,
By dat time, the cops are here;
I'm wishin' I'm down de corner
Sippin' a late nite beer.

Well, dis jerk had a gun, OK,
A big black toy from five and dime;
Wan black medic guy says
"Dis guy was once big time!"

De guy he still in coma, man;
De judge wait to see what comes;
I think I try and sell de store
And join dose crazy bums.

I always have my gun and bat;
Dis robber got a toy;
We both now got big problem, and
Dat ends dis sadshit story.

Morris and Saul

You either called them pianists
Or, you didn't call them at all;
The one with hair was named Morris
The other said, "Call me Saul."

They had an antique Steinway
In the old Cling Ting Café;
Don't ever get anywhere near it;
It was tuned almost every day.

They'd not been long in Shanghai,
Only since early in forty-two;
From Russia to Vienna and Milan;
The journey hard, if you were a Jew.

They lived and made a living,
In the place they called Hongkew;
The district had been made a ghetto
Where you must live, if you're a Jew.

Morris played '*Sentimental Journey*,'
And brought the GI's to tears;
Saul would opt for '*Liebestraum*'
(They were always shifting gears.)

Both had been concert divas,
They'd taught at the highest level;
Until they'd had to pack and go
And avoid the brute and the devil.

Some days they played a benefit,
But most every night they were on;
Starting around six or seven,
Sometimes they played until dawn.

"I only take one drink per hour,"
Saul once said to the crowd;
He would have been served one a minute
Had he not proclaimed this aloud

Much has been written about Shanghai,
And especially about Hongkew;
But, you had to be there to see it,
And feel it pulling at you.

The refugees from Germany and Poland
From Vienna and Russia, too;
No matter what their name was,
They came because it spelled Jew.

No, New York wouldn't take them,
Nor London, nor any other place;
No place they could make a living,
And know they would be safe.

The only port in all the world
That welcomed these refugees,
Was Shanghai, China, my friends,
And their hosts, the Sikhs and Chinese.

A Father's Advice

Women like to have babies,
Men like their wars;
Women like to cook and clean;
Sometimes men break laws.

Women like their Facebook
Men like to watch the game
Women like to dress and shop
Men like things the same.

Women like to be wanted and loved
It's just as simple as that;
So always keep your end up, son
And your union won't go flat.

Just in Case

I've known some guys
Who went to church
And some who even tithed;
Just in case, they said.

It wasn't that they didn't believe
It was more the question, 'of what'
And would it make much difference
Now they're finally dead?

One guy said it was like insurance
Plus, it made the wife feel good;
Especially Sunday mornings, when
They'd rather stay in bed.

Whimsey

Another one has gone ahead;
We called her Whimsey,
Cause that was her name,
And helping others
Was her game.

Husbands

Ever wonder why God made Husbands?
My wife's in a home with dementia,
With thirty-one other old timers;
That's why God made husbands.

The Home has ten or more women
For every man, you know,
And only a few, can say hello;
That's why God made husbands.

She cannot talk, and barely eats;
She cannot walk, or hold a spoon,
Wouldn't know the sun from a harvest moon;
But, that's why God made husbands.

Only her eyes will say hello, and
Each time I come through the door,
Her spirits, too, come alive, and soar;
That's why God made husbands.

Cookie and the Buffaloes

There's a place in India called Ledo,
About the size of Central Park,
It's the jumping off place for China;
Convoy Three now ready to embark.

One Hundred fifty trucks and so forth;
We'd stop at a half-way house, they said.
It would take us all day to get there;
By then, it'll be time for bed.

The half-way house was not to Kunming;
(Still a thousand miles away)
And this house they're talking about?
Well it's not a house, anyway!

Mountains and sky painted the windshield,
Unless you were dumb enough to look down;
Get out of the truck, you're walking up hill
On very un-solid ground.

Cookie had said he was a mountaineer, and
Would help us name the fauna and faun;
So after this goof ball strings his hammock,
He jumps in a jeep and is gone!

Harry Hart, the boxer cum doctor
Says, "I wonder where he's headed for;
There's tigers out there in the boonies
Maybe thinks he can find a cute whore?"

"No," said Cookie's driver, "he's cuckoo, and
He wants to bring down a buffalo;
Then tell the kids back home he's a hunter."
"Or maybe," says Harry, "a big hero."

Suddenly, one guy falls out of his hammock;
The boom, boom, was as loud as it can get;
It's coming from the trees up on the mountain
And Hart says, "That's Cookie; wanna bet?"

Cookie didn't shoot a buffalo, because
Right behind him and gaining fast
Was this king-sized leopard, or tiger
And neither looked happy, running past.

An Indian guide was watching all this, and
Laughing himself 'till he dropped;
Then he took two shots above the scene
And the whole thing came to a stop

We got a replacement for Cookie
A kid from East Tennessee;
He asked what happened to Cookie
Hart says, "Probably still up in that tree."

The Bunk Mate

Billy Joe talked to his pillow, every night;
I know, I was in the next bed;
But, he talked real soft, and sometimes
It was hard to catch what he said.

No question, he was scared as could be,
Not for himself, but his bride
Back there alone, pregnant and such;
One night he almost cried.

I kept it all in, and hoped he'd adjust
I wanted to tell the top-kick
Somebody had to help this guy;
He wasn't just lonely; he was sick.

Then, one night, about 2 AM,
He was up, and starting to pack;
I thought I'd yell, scare him a bit
Maybe get him back in the sack.

But, that was not an option,
Nor could I just make a grab;
Besides, we were in the middle of China;
What could he do? Call a cab?

But I laid there worrying
While he snuck out the back door;
Then I got up and dressed;
And started pacing the floor.

I had to do something, you see;
We're talking life and death;
So I finally sat down to think
And maybe catch my breath.

I must have dozed off;
Then I jumped off the chair,
Their was a shadow by the window,
Do I go out? Do I dare?

The door opens slowly, and
I'm in a really weird quandary;
Holy mackerel, it was Billie Joe
The guy had been doing his laundry

Lost in Burma

Middle of Burma, and not a murmur
From Ray as he shouldered his gun;
They both knew the cost of getting lost
"You said this was going to be fun."

I heard the noise, knew it wasn't the boys,
And said, "Maybe it's one of our Sikhs.
And maybe it's Grable screwing Gable,
Or a couple of Circus freaks."

Deep in the trees, and nary a breeze
Sweating like only one can
With a uniform on, and away since dawn
Just Roanoke Ray and me, Dan.

Just then, the groan, became a soft moan
And I almost lost my lunch;
We were too darn scared, and neither dared
But, wait! I've got a hunch!

I gave a little whistle, and through the thistle
A cute little lady was smiling;
"You melican guy, I knew by and by
You come out from where you hiding."

"I Burmese Nurse, here, see my purse
It have my name and license;
I go see convoy, and many soldier boy
Maybe I don't make some sense?"

So, Roanoke Ray put his M-1 away
And Dan was too stricken to speak;
He'd gone limp as a dove, and madly in love;
But alas, his whole body turned weak.

So, it came to pass that it couldn't last
He'd remember that smile forever;
Then he said good-bye, while wondering why
He can't think of something more clever.

But, just the same, he had her name
And maybe he could some day return
Then she turned away, he knew, some day
Was just another lesson to be learned.

The Ledo-Burma Road

Ledo is a small town in India; Kunming,
   In China and up 6000 feet;
In a six-by-six sat a one-eyed kid,
   In the old truck's shotgun seat.

The truck was one of about one-fifty,
   Loaded in Ledo, for Kunming
To supply the Chinese First Army;
   The kid said, "How do I load this thing?"

"Oh, shit, kid, you kidding me;
   You ain't never handled an M-One?"
   "Well, Lenny, I do payrolls;
   What would I do with a gun?"

"I heard Convoy 2 hasn't reached Kunming,"
   Lenny the sarge finally said,
"They got hung up in Myitkyina;
   I hope nobody's dead!"

The Captain said they got that far,
   And the fuckin' Japs were there;
Had to wait for the road to clear,
   But, nobody seemed to care.

The more matter of fact Lenny carried on,
   The hotter the cab seemed to get
He'd been on Convoy one, he said,
   And talked about a girl he had met.

But I gave the guy a luckie
And even dug out my lighter;
It seemed to slow him down a bit,
Maybe even quieter

"We'll only stay in Kunming two days,"
Said Lenny, "before they fly us back."
I could see he was on pins and needles
To get this gal in the sack.

We started before dawn the next morning,
And went straight up, it seemed,
Until we started weaving and sliding,
Worse than I'd ever dreamed.

"The first 100 miles is pretty bad;"
(We'd gone ten miles in two hours)
"We'll lose some trucks for sure," he said,
As I looked at the Himalayan towers.

On one side I could reach out and
Almost touch the walls of those hills;
If Lenny looked over his side of the truck,
He'd need some seasick pills.

Twelve days later we came out of the clouds,
And rolled on in to the city;
We lost an ambulance, two jeeps and a truck,
But were met by a nice committee!

First came a bath, and new uniforms;
We were promised the 'China Medal',
Then they showed us where not to go;
"Sure, Captain, you know we'll be careful!"

Love at First Sight

I was trolling Hongkew
With nothing to do,
And holding an over-night pass,
Then what do I see
Staring right at me
This cutie with one hell of an ass!

She was doing these tricks
(And getting her kicks,
As she watched the soldiers stroll by)
From her head to her toes
(Why, heaven only knows)
With a tall, skinny, Russian guy.

The guy had a baton
And a radio full on
Making music like you never heard;
She swayed and danced
(Sometimes she pranced)
Like some sort of mystical bird.

They had a small bucket
So I dropped in a nugget
A fistful of inflation's C-yen
When she caught my eye
I thought I would die,
Knowing I'd never see her again.

But, I was dead wrong
Because among the throng,
At the Cling Ting Café that night
(Morris was playing '*Blue Skies*,'
Delores was swatting blue flies,
I was higher than the proverbial kite.)

She was there in the far corner,
Like sitting in a sauna,
Was the girl I had seen in Honkew.
She was wearing short shorts,
Like you see at tennis courts,
So, now, what the hell do I do?

I could maybe go book her;
(She was most likely a hooker);
Then Saul gave a tap on my shoulder;
"She's waiting for you," he said
"But she's not ready to bed;
She's a small keg of ice, even colder."

Yep, this was Shanghai, 1945
One minute dead, the next alive;
Refugees from the crowded Hongkew,
Little coolies hugging Sikhs
Parties lasting for many weeks;
Russian, French, and German Jews.

Of course, Saul had been lying
And I knew that he was crying
For this girl I saw in the Old Quarter.
Then later I heard, from another guy
Why Saul the Pianist had to try;
The cutie in shorts was his daughter.

Fenway Park

I'd like to stroll
Around Fenway Park
Some night when it's snowing,
And really dark.

I want to hear
What goes on with the ghosts;
And I want to lift
A few goodbye toasts.

Not so much
To the Teds and the Groves,
But to the unknown kids,
Who came in droves.

They numbered in millions
But they're not on the wall;
They just came to see
Their heroes play ball.

I want to tell them
I can hear the crying;
Because it looks like
The new guys aren't trying.

But, this too will pass
A new day will come;
And next year we'll be beating
A brand new drum!

I had written this sometime during the winter of 2003-2004. If you are a Red Sox fan, you'll know what happened the following year.

Concealed Weapons

I got out of my car at the grocery store,
Shut the engine and slammed the door;
Then I happened to see, almost next to me.
A big black van under a cypress tree.

The van was half hidden, maybe never moved,
Supposed to be a sign, in a spot approved
By the grocery store, or maybe the city;
Strange, I thought, and not very pretty.

As I walked on by, headed for the store,
My eye caught the sign on the driver's door,
It read, 'CONCEALED WEAPONS CLASSES'.
I stopped in my tracks, and checked my glasses.

No, that's what it said, and now I was sure
How I could get out of being poor;
All I needed was the gun, and that permit,
And I could get out of this life of shit.

Well I got the gun by waylaying a cop
Who was checking back doors at a donut shop,
Then I called CWS and took the exam,
Paid with a check from another scam.

Last night I drove to Clearwater Bay;
Did a couple of cabbies while on the way.
One of them reached for a gun (that was bad)
I put a bullet in his shoulder (he'd made me mad.)

Since they said it was OK to carry my new gun
I'm really having lots of fun, and wondering
Who thought up those wonderful classes
And got us sad sacks up off our asses.

This Old Plane

"Nothing to do with you Bob
I think they were glad to oblige;
They cheered when I asked for the transfer."
The top-kick said in a whisper.

"We're stuck in India, not much doing
You might as well be in Kunming;
Here, we got the mosquitoes
Plus the heat we'll get in the spring."

They loaded me on, with about 20 others,
To a broken down C-43;
It had no doubt made a thousand safe trips;
But, this one was going to take me.

So, fifty or so miles from Kunming Field
It suddenly turns almost quiet;
There still was a hum from one engine
(But, I saw no signs of a riot.)

In fact, and to the surprise of us all,
The co-pilot looked back and said,
"Sorry, fellas, but this old broad
Belongs in a museum shed."

He went on, "Sit tight while Sammy feathers
The engine that's out there smoking;
We'll find a paddy near the road;
We thought the guy was joking!"

And that's what they did,
The two pilots up front;
They put us down in a rice paddy,
The nose taking most of the brunt.

"The roads over there guys,
About half a mile away;
Let's hope there's a new convoy
Coming by some day."

Sure enough, it wasn't that long
So we visited a village nearby;
They gave us pancakes and rice wine;
We all hated to say good bye!

We asked the pilot about the crash;
Can you tell us what went wrong?
"Sure," Sammy said for all to hear
"She's been out here too damn long!"

Dr. Lasky

Sometime in the fall of thirty-nine
A doctor named Lasky left the U.S.;
Setting sail for Shanghai, China;
Him being in a terrible mess.

He'd been disbarred for mal-practice;
("Abortions for rape victims," he said.)
The Medical Board of Ohio
Was incensed, and 'after my fucking head'!

But, he was allowed to practice in China
Times were tough enough there all ready;
What with the Japs taking over,
They were not going to be too picky.

Lasky had barely started his practice,
When Tojo's boys came around;
He wound up in a round-up
Of every round-eye in town.

Now, in this 'visitors' compound,'
The Doctor made many good friends
Among them some Mao Zedong guys
In a courtyard while doing knee bends.

He noticed these guys had wristbands
And attached were pieces of jade;
He asked why the Japs didn't take them?
They said, "'cause they're deathly afraid."

Lasky realized they were the 'healing stones'
That he'd heard about at OSU;
He thought it was crazy quack medicine,
But was ready to learn something new.

And he also heard about burial suits,
Made out of nephrite jade;
But they said, "Don't hold your breath, Doc,
There were only a very few made."

So, in mid-September, 1945,
Lasky was free to roam;
He was hired by the US Army
And, voila, he'd found a new home

But, alas, that didn't last too long either;
Because soon, the Americans were gone,
Chaing was out, Mao was in and
Communist China was re-born

For years, nobody heard from the doctor;
He'd written a few letters in 'forty-six,
But they were always weeks in transit,
And addressed to me, at Fort Dix.

And then one night at a Christy's auction,
In late August, nineteen eighty-eight
I'm sitting watching the action
And there he is, my old mate!

Lost in Burma

Two rows down, and on the aisle,
A China Beauty, snug on his right;
Now, it's long ago, forty plus years
And it gave me one hell of a fright.

Then damned if Lasky didn't turn around,
And wave at my wife and me;
He must have seen us arrive, I guess,
And I wondered how this could be.

It was obvious old Lasky had prospered;
He looked like he really had it made
When we got together after the sale, he said,
"Wanna buy some healing jade?"

Where Are You

"Hi, jus leevin Dunkin
Gotta run, tk in morn."
"Lyin basta, U over at Lenas
Watchin more stupid porn."

Reggie shook his head, and
Hit the button to End;
Thinking, "Why do I do this
To another good old friend?"

That was a dozen texts ago;
They trailed him around all day;
Half sent silly pictures
One sent a message, "Let's pray."

Reg remember being so excited
The day he got his pad
Who knew he'd never read
Another good book---how sad!

Celebrating the Big Nine-O

Woke up this morning
Couldn't quit yawning;
Then realized what day it was
Checked a calendar
(Just took a gander)
And quickly got a hot buzz.

Actually got flighty
From turning ninety
(Lemme see if all is still there)
Tools all in place
A nose on the face
Wow! Even a little white hair!

So, I'm quitting activities
And certain festivities
That might hasten the inevitable end
No more 2 packs of Luckys'
Or fifths of Kentuckys'
(At least, that's what I intend!)

One of these Days

'One of these days'
Get's closer all the time;
Some organ or another
May just stop on a dime

Your balance is lost
At the top of the steps
(Do you remember
When you counted reps?)

Ever heard of people
Who went to bed?
Saying, 'fuck it!',
And woke up dead?

But, the humidity is down,
The sun is shining;
The Sox won again
So, why am I whining?

The Five and Dime

The kid had a nickel for each of his years,
Burning a hole in his pocket.
The day before Christmas, he's thinking,
"My Mom would love a nice locket."

Now it's nearly a mile to downtown Keene
From his house on Dover Street;
And it's way below freezing, but jeepers,
How else do I get her a treat?

So off the kid trots in the slush and snow
With feet getting squishy, cold and wet;
He's almost there at the five and dime
And it'll soon be dark, but not yet.

Now this is the winter of 'twenty-nine
Wall Street came totally unglued;
Some guys are jumping off buildings;
The others are getting sued.

It's three years before election
And some order was finally restored;
Banks had to close, and not for a day
The guy on the street was ignored.

The kid got to the store and asked the lady
"I'd like a locket for my Mom,
And I've got 25 cents I can spend,
But I know it's not a great sum."

Ten minutes later, with the store closing down,
The boy walked out with a gift box,
And holding the hand of the store cop;
While admiring his brand new knee socks.

The policeman, while still on duty,
Walked the kid home to his mother,
Who almost feinted away, because
She thought I was with my brother!

Mr. Fowler

The Vice-Principal stood in front of our class
And we all got a little nervous;
It meant another teacher was going
Into some military service.

The year was nineteen-forty one;
The month was late December;
So many teachers left our school,
Some, I'll always remember.

Fourteen months later, I too would go
But those first guys were special
They were college, they were mature
They'd be officers, maybe a general.

Fowler was my English teacher,
Mr. Giroux said, "He left today,
I guess to be a bomber pilot;
At least that's what they say."

Mr. Fowler got me interested
In poets like Shelley and Keats;
I even did a report on 'Invictus'
(My most memorable English feat.)

By the time I headed overseas,
Both my brother and my teacher were down
Dick in the South Pacific
Mr. Fowler was never found

My brother came back, but didn't last
His body had taken too much;
But many nights I wake up and pray,
That maybe some day we can touch.

I'm not a religious person
And I will soon be on my way;
But I haven't the slightest fear
Of any judgment day.

Maybe (perhaps) I could change my mind
(I haven't been there before.)
Meanwhile, it's nice to dream and wonder,
Who might open the Golden Door.

Shanghai: October 1945

Shanghai, China nineteen forty-five
A fractured metropolis comes alive;
Colors range from the darkest Sikh
To the Whitish Russian, Brit, or Greek.

Enemies walk around, guns on backs
Lugging their stuff in gunny-sacks.
"Where we go soldier? You know?"
"Where we leave guns? Please, you show?"

Coolies bow to the Sikhs, the Sikhs to us,
Who ever they are, they're in a rush
To trade some dollars, get some C-Yen
While the stuff is hot, and a dollar brings ten.

But, in just a few hours, a brand new scene;
The rate of exchange has jumped to fifteen!
It seems there's a kiosk near every hotel,
And some would-be Genie has rung the bell.

Meanwhile the GI's are making the rounds,
And the gin mill signs say, "dollars or pounds;"
The Park Hotel took most of our batch
(The place next door was called 'Down the Hatch')

Well, we wound up living where we'd labor,
And, boy, did the generals do us a favor;
They stuck us in Honkew (of all the places)
And, in about two seconds, we're off to the races!

Just down the street it's like Mardi Gras
A place called Bohemia has a 20 foot bar;
And two Russian refugees, musicians supreme
Who played different styles, but both like a dream.

On a stool near the bar, Natasha held court
Singing '*Sentimental Journey*' while drinking her port;
But only while Bennie was tinkling the keys;
(To Morris that stuff was nothing but sleaze)

I left for the States in early December
And how could I ever, not remember?
The whole scene might not have lasted long;
(We knew Chiang Kai-shek did everything wrong.)

So civil wars broke out all around,
And the China we knew went deep underground;
Yet, I'd like to see China, just once more,
Take a walk through Honkew, just like before.

But with no one to share an adventure,
(My dear wife has been taken by dementia)
And my old war buddies, damaged or dead,
I guess I'll just have another cookie,
and get myself to bed.

Ninety, Come and Gone

Zipped on past ninety,
Like it wasn't even there;
Some say, you're how old, Bob?
Most don't really care.

Not awfully religious
Still, nobody's really certain
'Cept what will be, will be
Behind the cloudy curtain.

Two wives already there;
Hope they found each other;
And also with their children
Moms, dads, my big brother.

I can't help thinking
How will they greet me?
Guess I can hope;
Be interesting, don't you see?

Two Dollar Bill

Let me tell you about Two Dollar Bill,
Our corner bookie and pal;
He'd been on that corner for ever
He and his buddy, young Sal.

Then came the day he went missing;
That stretched into two or three;
And everyone started talking
Like, "Where the hell could he be?"

Well, to make this story short (but not so sweet)
They finally called it dementia
And Two Dollar Bill was headed
For a not-too-happy-adventure.

He was placed in this home not far away,
And one day I went out to see him;
In a powered chair; while combing his hair
Was a real pretty lady he called Kim.

Now Two Dollar Bill couldn't recall my name,
But knew I was someone he knew
So he asked me if I wanted a ticket;
Or, maybe even a few.

It seems that Bill kept his hand in;
Like, selling tickets to whomever
In a rather unique kind of lottery
(Talk about a clever endeavor!)

Each ticket bore a room number;
(Yes, they cost two bucks a pop)
And if your resident was next to go
Why, you won the lottery pot!

Political Junkies

Raymond Monk was a political junkie
(His Mom once called Hoover a 'punkie')
Which was not a surprise,
She once got a rise,
For calling her Ray, 'little monkey'.

Well, Ray understood his mommy
Hadn't he been yanked from her tummy?
She read to him about Frankie
Who never seemed to get cranky
(Unless he was losing at rummy)

But it was Truman whom she loved
Her Harry, (neither hawk nor dove);
The guy who had pulled the trigger
With the bomb that was so damn much bigger
(Was it Doug who gave him the shove?)

But now Ray has given it up, you see;
Where's the new Franklin D.?
The Demos are dumb, the Reps even worse,
He thinks they're all under some wicked curse;
Another ten years, and what will we be?

The Senator

Senator Zits was a tubby old Mick;
Dumb Irish, from bottom to top;
But, Old Zits was as slick
As a garbage man's boot,
And sneaky as a county cop.

Please don't ask me why this little ditty is in with the good stuff. The man's name isn't Zits, and he was a Representative, not a Senator, but he is a friend, and wanted to see the 'poem' in print!

About the Author

Robert E. Maloney was the first person in his family to be born in a hospital (Keene, NH---1924). He served in the US Army from March 1943 until December 1948. Uncle Sam happily provided passage, with beer and cigarette money, to some exotic places like, Bombay and Ledo (India), Bhamo and Lashio (Burma), and Kunming and Shanghai (China). Thanks to the GI Bill, he received two degrees (Industrial Engineering and Engineering Management) from Northeastern University.

He married two wonderful women, both now deceased. He made a decent living, enjoyed spending most of it, as a mechanical engineer (during the cold war) and as a conniving stockbroker during the roaring eighties. His children are up north swatting bugs and cursing the New England and New York traffic.

He has another book due out on the heels of this one. It is a trio titled, *A WORLD WAR II TRILOGY*. He expects it to outsell *FROM HERE TO ETERNITY*, and says, "If it doesn't, at this stage of my game (age 90), who will give a damn one way or the other.

Connect with Robert

Robert's Publisher

http://SpiderBooksPublishing.com

Robert's Facebook

https://www.facebook.com/bob.maloney.315

Robert's Website

www.ingramcontent.com/pod-product-compliance
Lightning Source LLC
Chambersburg PA
CBHW071018040426
42443CB00007B/829